a KALEIDOSCOPIA coloring booK

ABSTRACT ADVENTURE XI

Created by Kendall Bohn

Abstract Adventure XI

Published by Kaleidoscopia Coloring Books

Kaleidoscopia Coloring Books, 2205 California Street NE Suite #300, Minneapolis, MN 55418

Printed in the United States of America on Acid-free paper.

Visit KaleidoscopiaColoringBooks.com for our full selection of coloring books designed with you in mind. Autographed copies are available.

KaleidoscopiaColoringBooks.com

9 of the 52 images

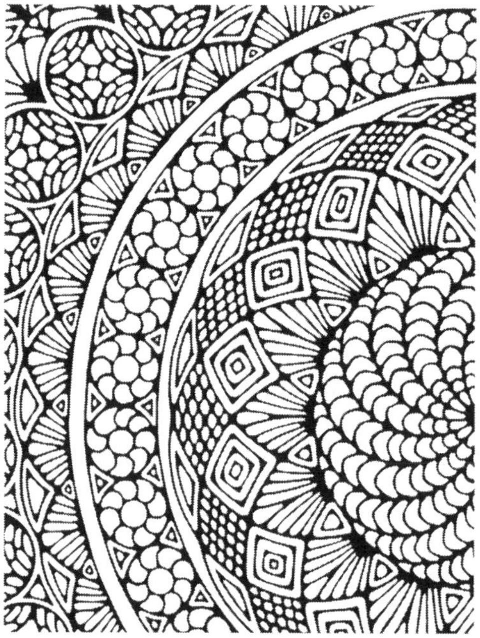
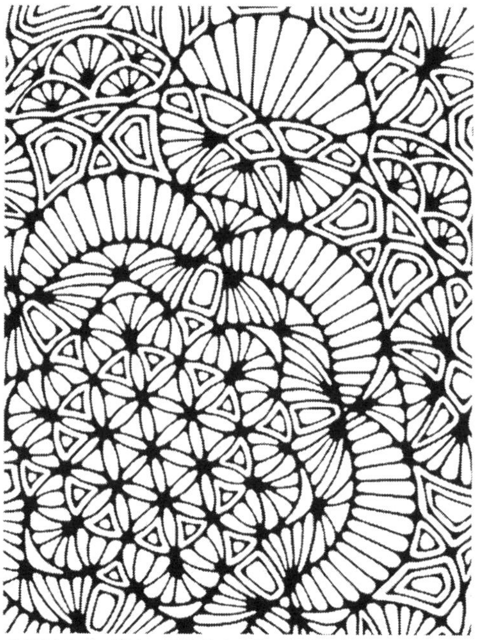
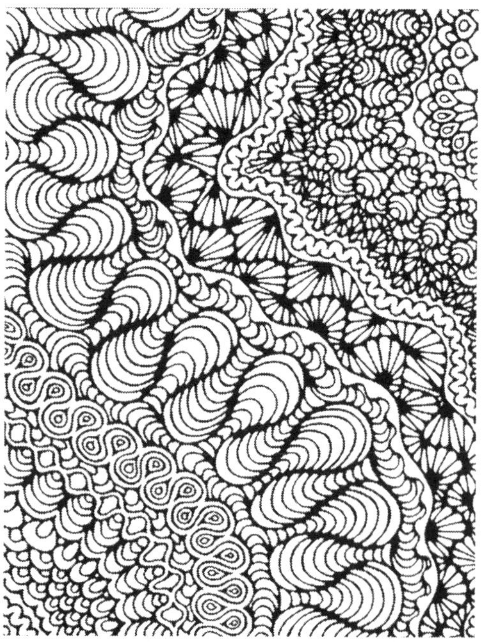
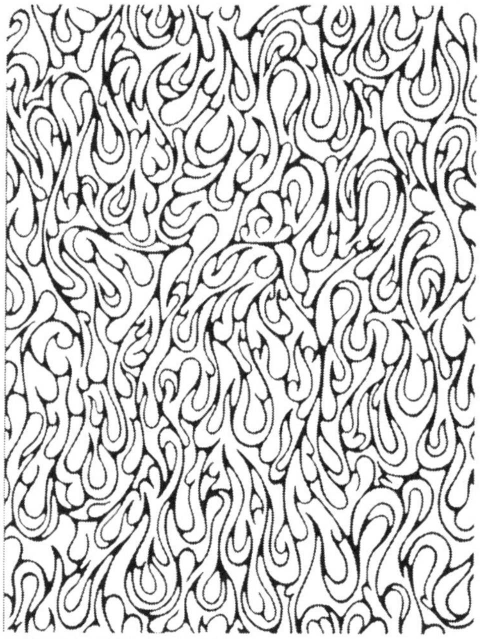
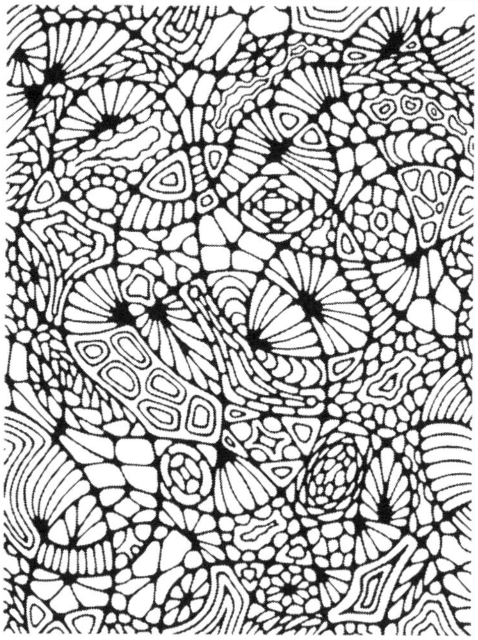
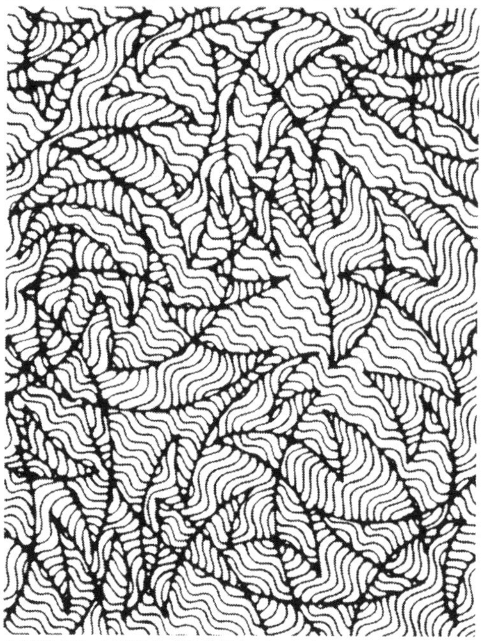
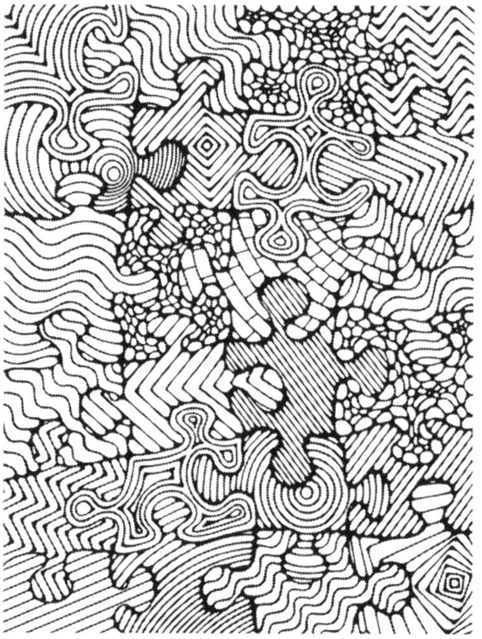
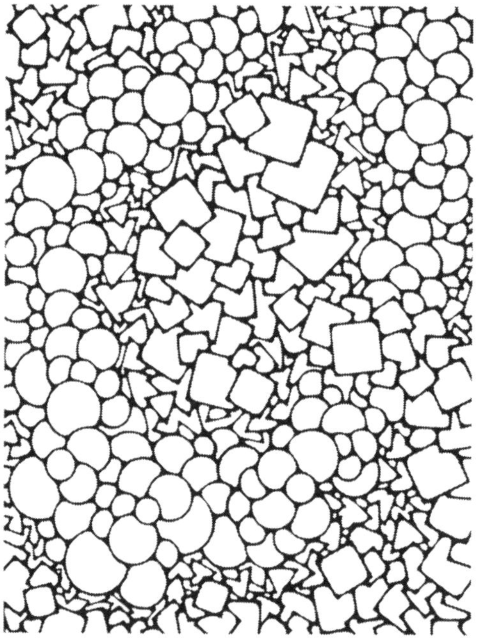
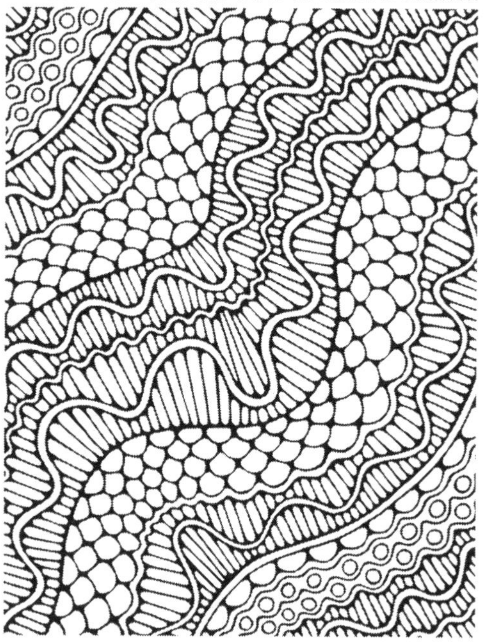

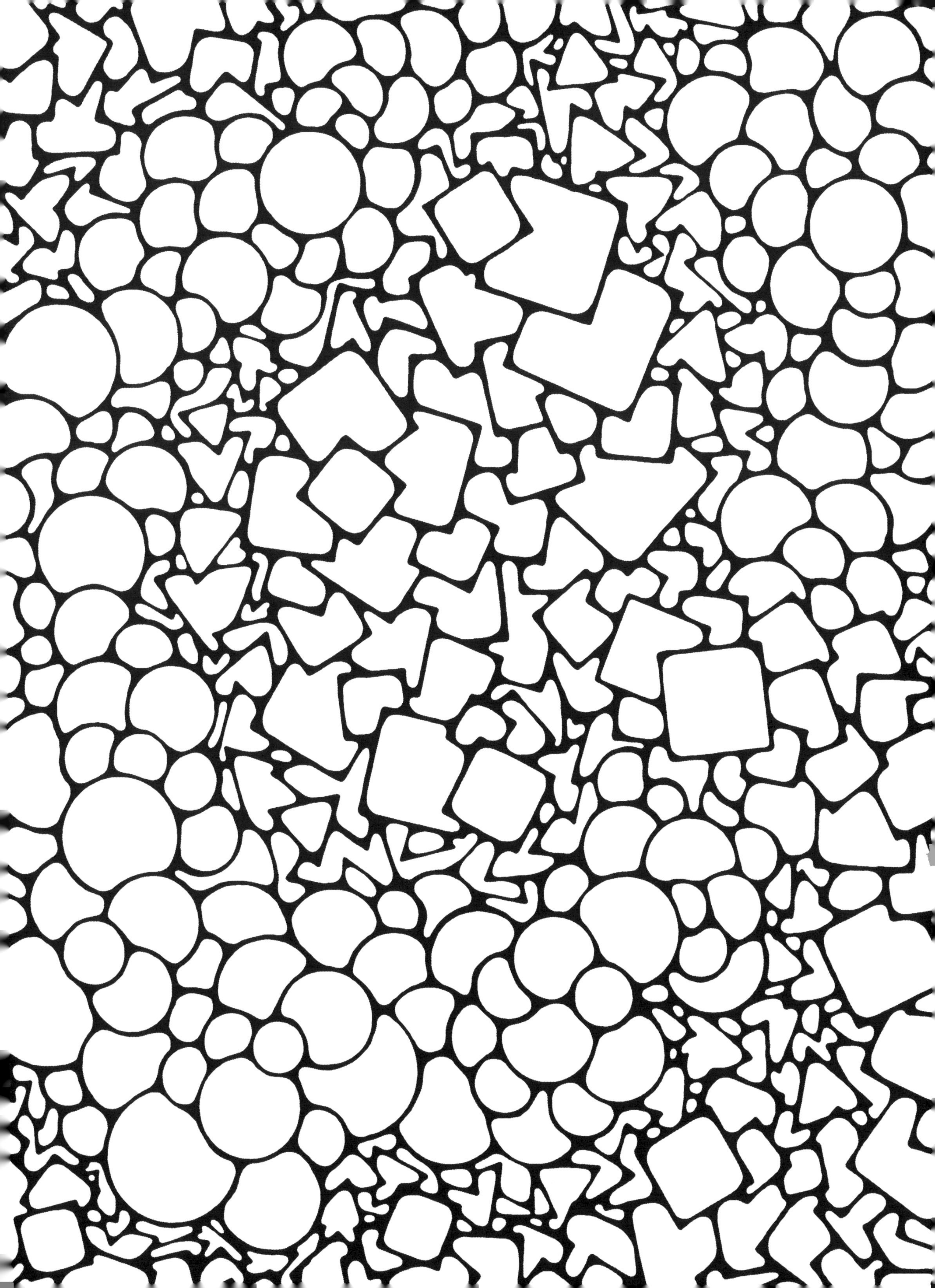

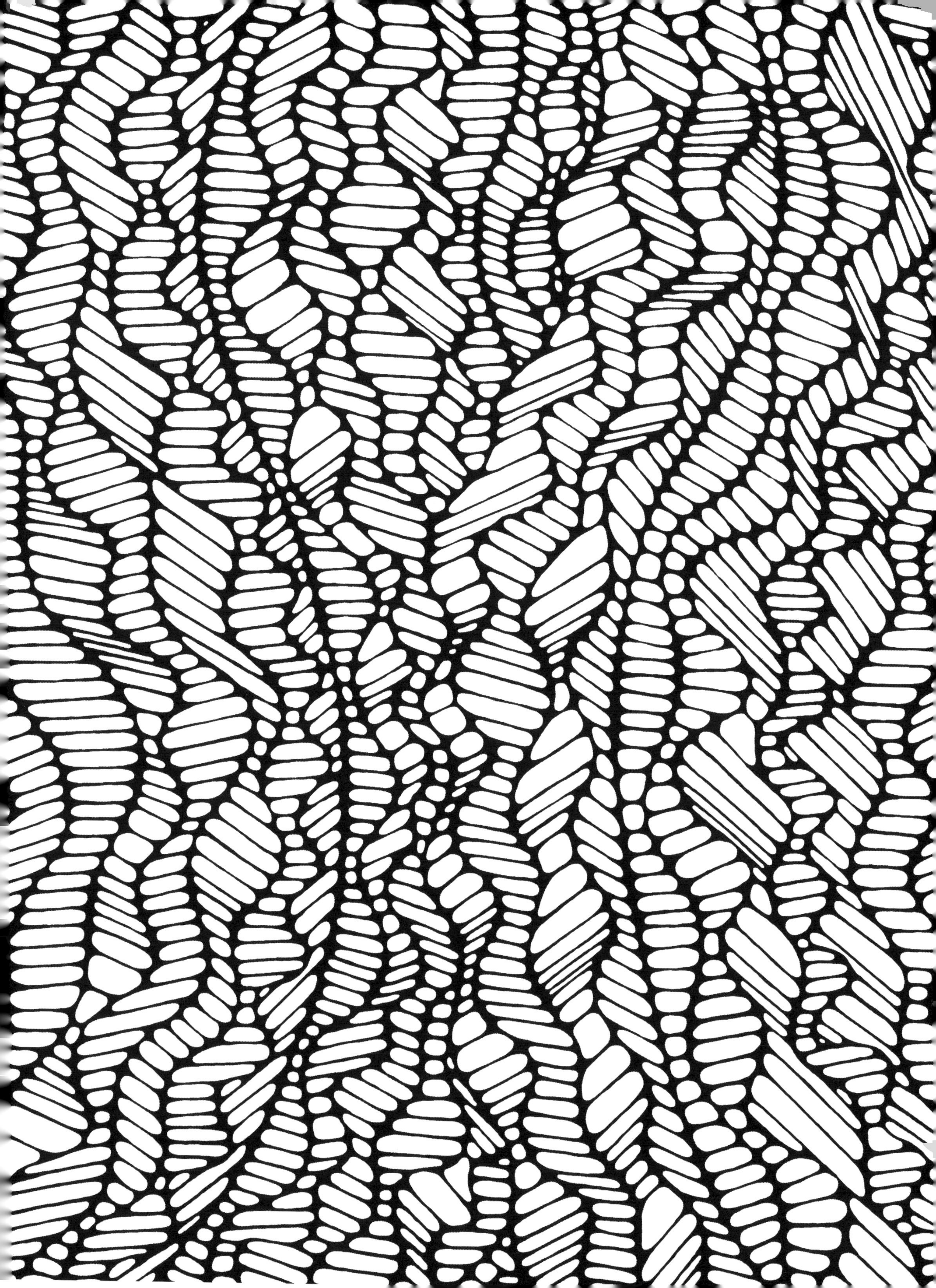

Color Wheel

Color Wheel: The arrangement of colors in a circle, showing the relationships between the primary and secondary colors.

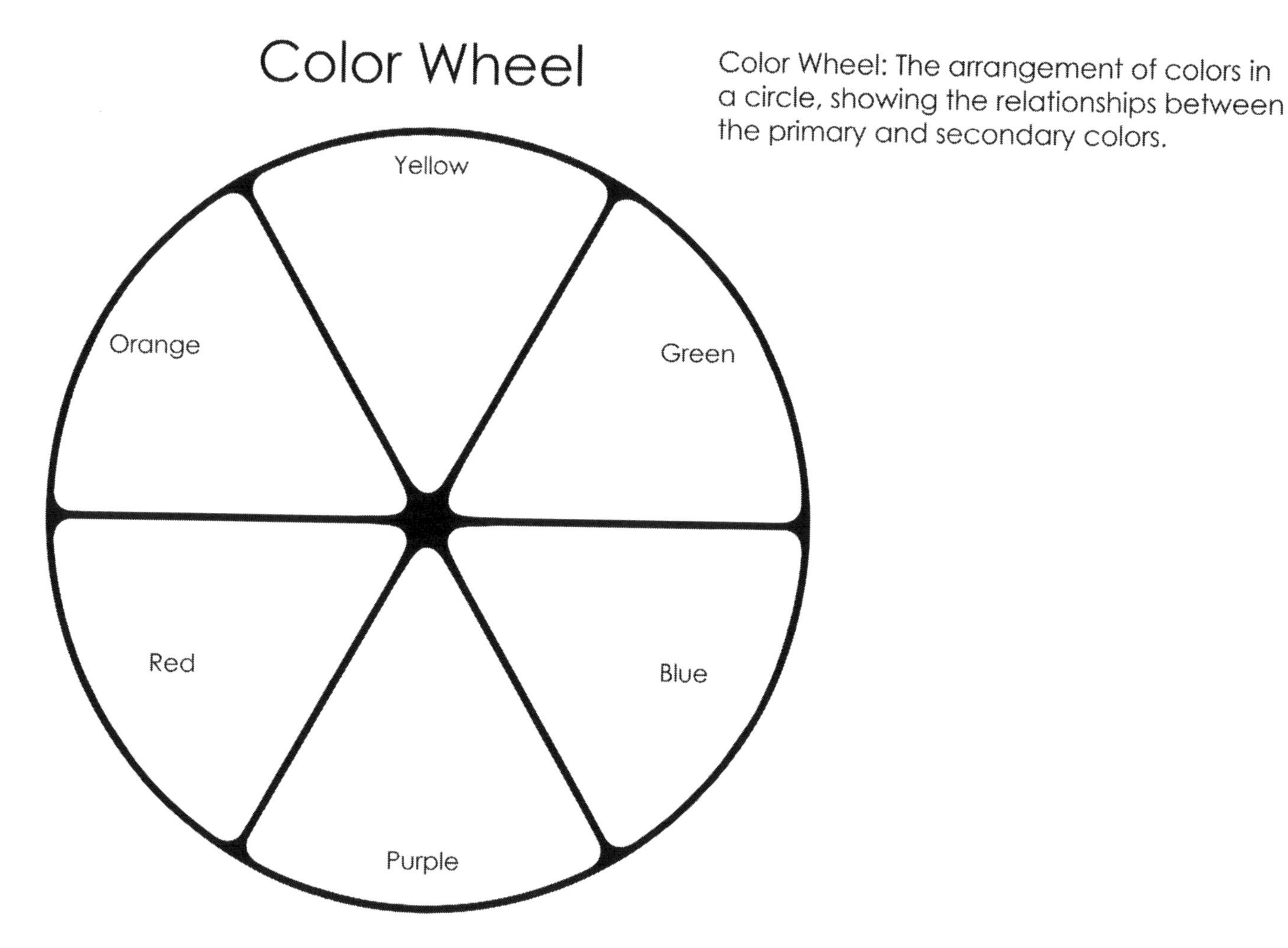

Primary Colors: Red, Blue and Yellow. These colors cannot be created by mixing the secondary colors.

Secondary Colors: Green, Orange and Purple. These colors are made by mixing two of the primary colors: Red + Blue = Purple, Blue + Yellow = Green, Yellow + Red = Orange.

primary colors

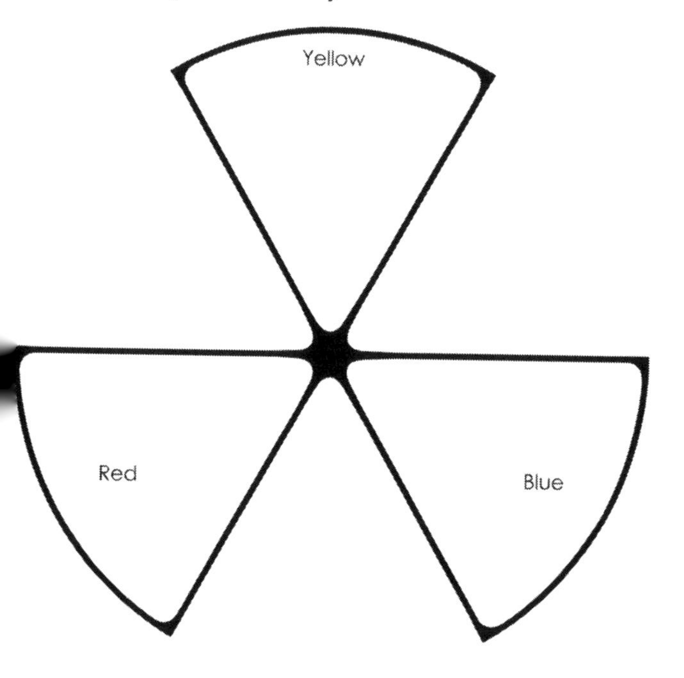

secondary colors

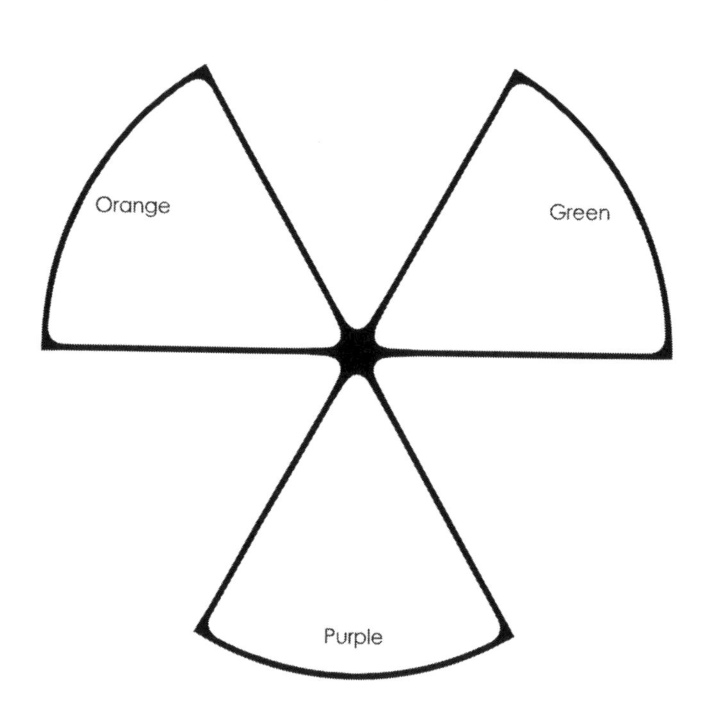

Introduction to color: Refer to color wheel and value scale on back cover.

Color Wheel: The arrangement of the color spectrum that shows the relationship between colors.

Hue: This term is used to describe the purest form of any color, such as Yellow, Orange, Red, Purple, Blue or Green.

Primary Colors: Red, Blue and Yellow. These colors cannot be created by mixing other colors.

Secondary Colors: Green, Orange and Purple. These colors are made by mixing two of the primaries: Red + Blue = Purple Blue + Yellow = Green Yellow + Red = Orange.

Triad Colors: Any three hues that are the same distance apart.

Tertiary Colors: Created by mixing a primary color and an adjacent secondary color. *Example:* Yellow-Green, Blue-Green, Violet-Blue, Violet-Red, Red-Orange and Yellow-Orange. There are endless variations of tertiary colors, depending on how much of one hue and another are mixed.

Complementary: Any two colors straight across from each other on the color wheel. *Example*: Red/Green, Blue/Orange and Purple/Yellow. When color opposites are used next to each other the extreme contrast makes the image pop. They create excitement in the design. *Example*: In a purple background with a yellow shape on it, the yellow will jump off the page.

Analogous Colors: Any three colors that are right next to each other on the color wheel. *Example*: Violet Blue, Blue, Blue Green. These schemes work well together to create a flowing harmony for easy transitions from one color to the next as well as a peaceful feeling in the design .

Value: Refers to how light or dark a color is.

Shade: Adding black or a darker hue to a color. The more black a color has, the darker its value.

Tint: Adding white or a lighter hue to a color. The more white a color has, the lighter its value.

Tone: A hue mixed with a neutral color, a gray or brown.

Warm Colors: Red, Yellow, and Orange. These colors remind us of the sun or fire.

Cool Colors: Blue, Green, and Purple. These colors remind us of water, sky or grass.

Neutral Colors: Grays and Browns. Gray is made by mixing White & Black. Browns are made by mixing complementary colors or all three primary colors. These neutral colors or earth tones are dirty and dull. When used with pure hues they become more vibrant.

Discord Colors: are colors of the same value placed together. These color combinations are visually disturbing. They clash causing a painful vibrating sensation. However unpleasant it may be this negative feeling can provide an exciting reaction. You create discord by raising or lowering the values of hues until they are the same. Such as adding white to a blue, purple or red until it is the same value as yellow.

Split Complementary Colors: This scheme uses a color and the two colors next to its complement. *Example*: Yellow with Red Violet and Blue Violet. This creates contrast without the strong tension of the extreme opposites.

Double Complementary or Tetradic Colors: This scheme uses four colors so it has the greatest variety of combinations. The colors are chosen from any two contrasting color pairs. *Example*: Red/Green and Blue/Orange. This color scheme may look out of balance and may be difficult to harmonize if the four are used in equal amounts. To achieve balance and harmony in the image the colors need to be adjusted by changing their value, tone, and/or amount.

Made in the USA
Lexington, KY
17 March 2016